Petals Snowfall

published haiku and
original art by Elena Malec

2022

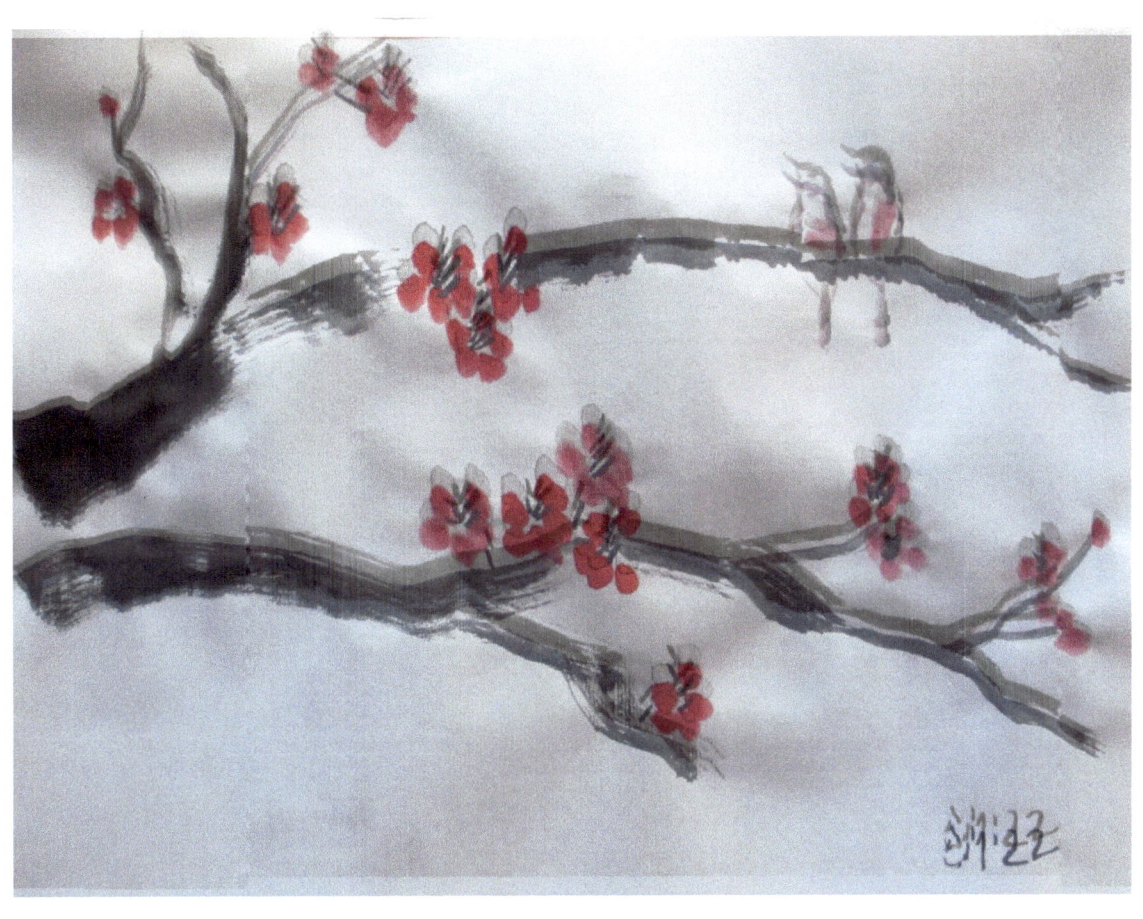

dry straw for grabs
pair of swallows
with a purpose

HaikUniverse - April 10, 2022

---

behind the front lines
swallowtail resting
on a blue and yellow kite

Haiku Dialogue - April, 27, 2022

---

rose water drink
getting younger
with every cup

brass bell haiku journal - May issue 2022

May Day
the queen celebrates
the worker bees

Cold Moon Journal - May 1, 2022

---

sap green leeks
the watercolor tube
almost empty

Haiku Dialogue - May, 5 2022

----

single branch ikebana . . .
shadows of furry catkins
on an empty wall

Charlotte Digregorio Writer's blog - May 7, 2022

----

sweet lilac scent
blooms tucked away
in Mom's bosom

Haiku Dialogue - May 11, 2022

----

wedding plans
in the mailbox
a ladybug

Stardust haiku issue 65, May 27, 2022

----

rosemary-
the aroma of your name
on Sunday roast

scrambled eggs-
making the mess in your life
fluffy

rum ice cream
Havana
on my mind

The failed haiku, June 1, 2022 issue 78

---

dandelion fluff
my illusions blown
by the north wind

featured in Haiku corner, Haiku of the week, Week 17- 9-13 May 2022

---

swallowtail resting-
collecting my thoughts
among wildflowers

Haiku corner- May 24, 2022

---

swarm of bees-
perfuming the entire street
old acacia tree

Haiku corner - June 1, 2022

filled to the brim with emptiness origami cup

deep meditation a fly fell asleep on my forehead

brass bell haiku journal - June issue 2022

---

roles
choosing between king
and joker

Cold Moon Journal - June 2, 2022

---

her chiffon tutu
courtship ritual
of white flamingos

Scarlet Dragonfly Journal - June 2, 2022

---

snail way
what is
the rush

Haiku corner - June 7, 2022

---

haiku postcard
a ladybug climbing
the peony stamp

Haiku Dialogue - June 15, 2022

---

collector frustration
snatching the net
off the lilac bush

Asahi Haikuist Network
June 17, 2022

---

blooming sakura -
swans on the pond
carrying petals

Autumn Moon Haiku Journal
June 17, 2022

---

acacia in bloom
little girl feeding sweet flowers
to her dolls

Haiku corner - June 21, 2022

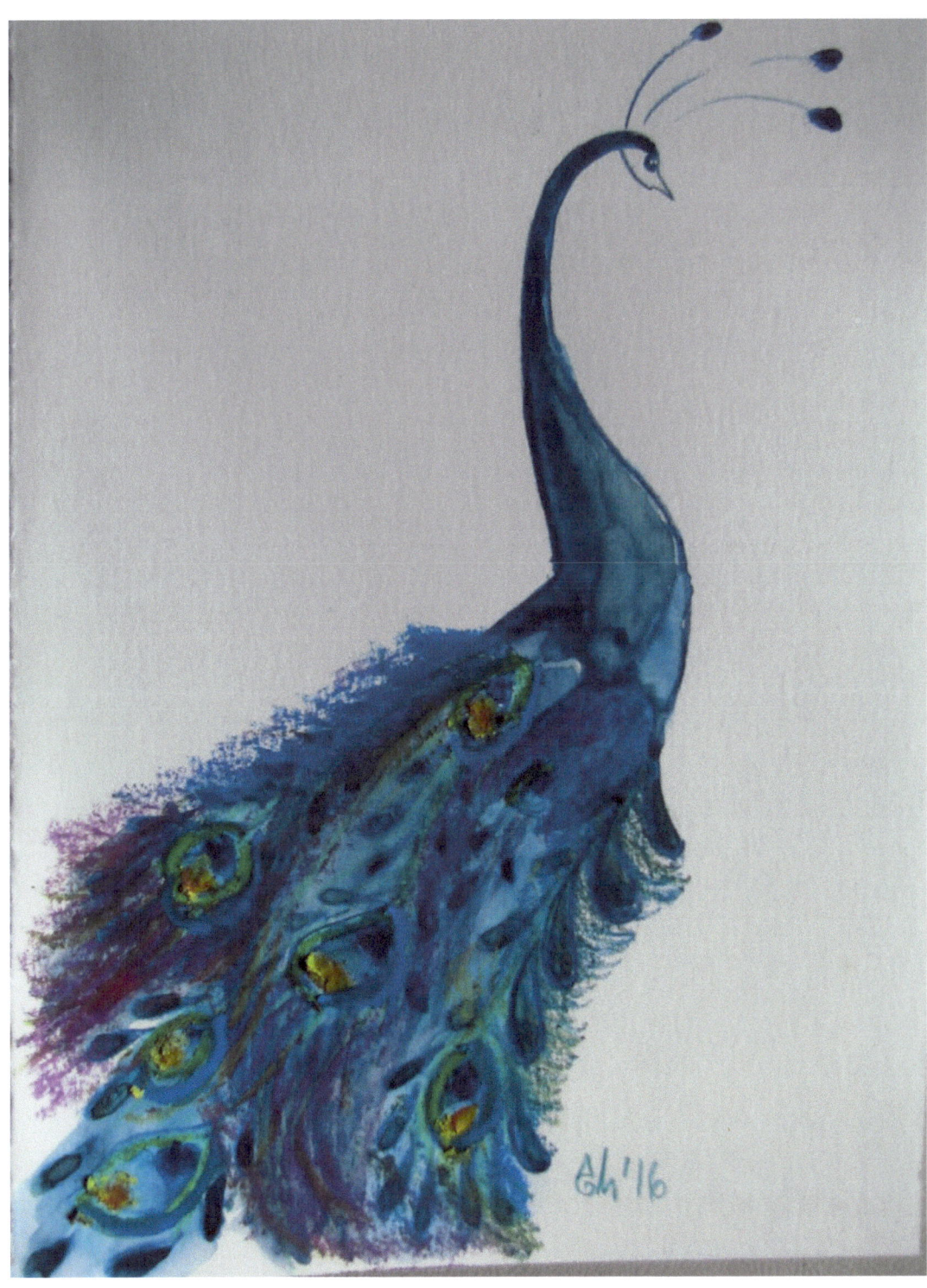

first anniversary
nothing to say but
a red carnation

Haiku Dialogue - June 21, 2022

---

solo guitar
living on a shoestring
budget

Cold Moon Journal - June 30, 2022

---

gin flavor
my husband is into botanicals
too

Tsuri-doro issue - 10 July August, 2022

---

flying
with no sound
origami plane

brass bell haiku journal – July 2022

Editor's Choice
a haiku about peace
in every issue

Asahi Haikuist Network - July 1st, 2022

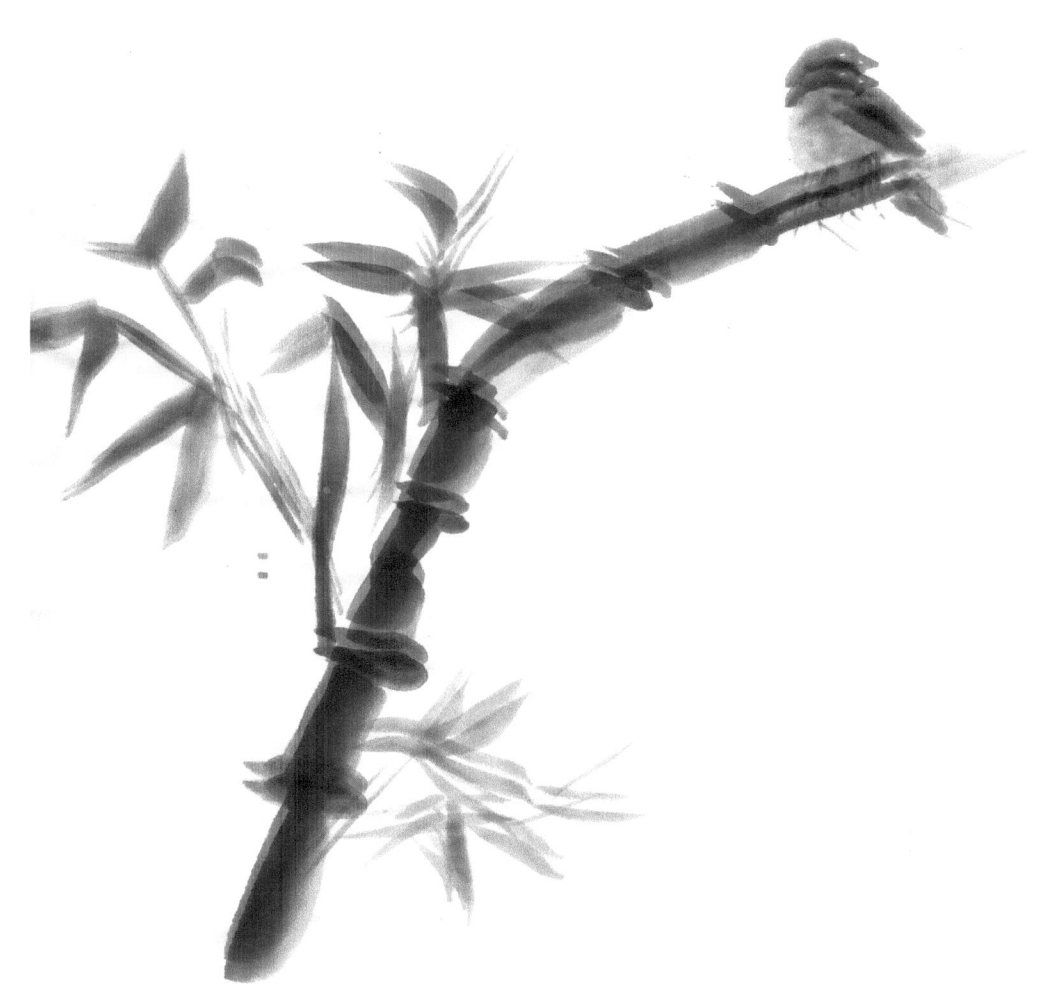

pomegranate seeds
another blissful year
together

Haiku Dialogue - July 6, 2022

---

shadow play
our heroes
but cardboard cutouts

pink cotton candy stick
sunset colors
on loose cumulus

torrid days
the watermelon water
dripping down my chin

silent ritual
a monarch
in a daisy field

petals snowfall
fragrant acacia
marking its territory

The Zen Space- July 8, 2022

hopscotch
blowing off chalk and lime
summer storm

Scarlet Dragonfly Journal- July 19, 22

---

homeless man sleeping under bridge
the north wind blowing
fallen maple leaves

Plum Tree Tavern - July 25, 2022

-----

after sixty-five
trying envy
for a change

Plum Juice Journal of Senryu - July 31, 22

fish bowl
in the cat's iris
a guppy

brass bell haiku journal - Aug. 1st, 2022

vibrant sunset
the mix on my palette
fiery

Haiku corner- Aug. 17th, 2022

I come alive
the cry of seagulls
at dawn

Scarlet Dragonfly Journal – September 1, 2022

---

somewhere in bucharest
the apricot tree
my childhood hideout

brass bell haiku journal – September 1, 2022

---

cut up watermelon
sunset sky sinking
into the ocean

Cold Moon Journal, September 24, 2022

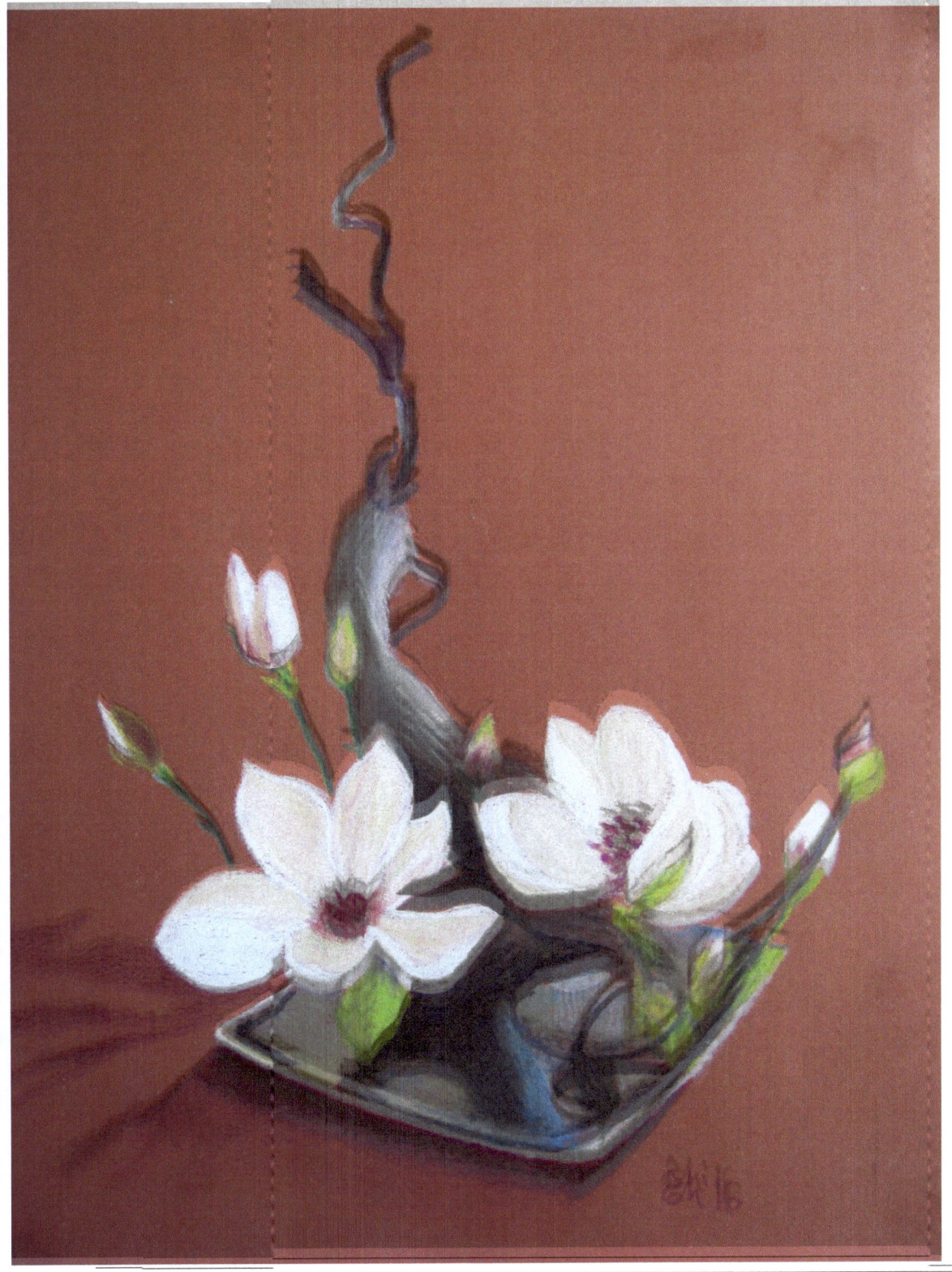

rainy weather
champignons a la crème
everyday

brass bell haiku journal – October 1, 2022

----

shooting offseason
geese flying
in sunset colors

Asaki Haikuist Network – October 6, 2022

----

windy city
off-key saxophone
grating the night

Tsuri-doro – October 30, 2022

----

my life so far unfolding exquisite scars

brass bell haiku journal – November 1, 2022

----

steaming tea
the cat's whiskers pierce
the frigid air

autumn sky
the sound of rain
on a tortoise shell

chrysanthemum leaves
the scent of approaching
winter

The Bamboo Hut – November 14, 2022

---

night book fair
so many styles
of mythmaking

brass bell haiku journal, December 1, 2022

---

night holiday market
a mistletoe twig
left behind

Autumn Moon Journal – December 8, 2022

---

guitar lessons
my youth
an improvisation

tinywords – December 26, 2022

---

late fall orchard -
fluffing up feathers
sparrows sustain the sky

Cold Moon Journal, December 31, 2022

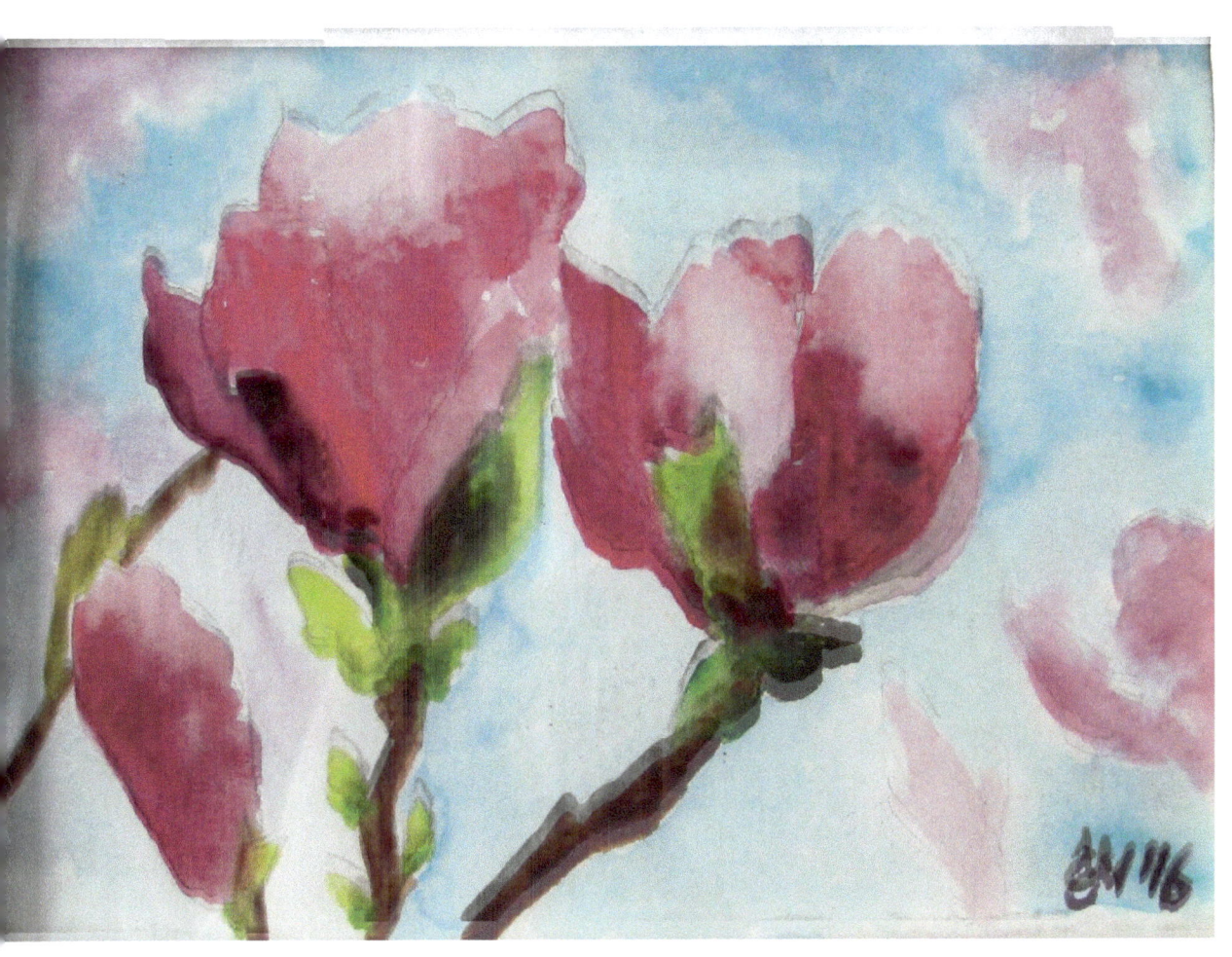

Other Haiku

shards of mirror
gathering suns from the ground
and pieces of sky

peony bouquet
young bride blushing
under the veil

wild mustard field
a treat for
the busy bees

herbes de Provence
floral overtones
of dried lavender

dried basil flowers
casting love spells
village girl

bossanova night
tropical beats
in your passion

lavender bundle
tying me up
with your love

cranes flying south
a lone feather
swinging in the air

scattered straw
scarecrow patched coat
in tatters

first fluffy snowflakes
croaking crows flight
over the frozen field

watercolor brushes
Christmas tree greener
in the cat's eyes

tundra frosts
still moon
in reindeer's eyes

train station departure
your handkerchief
a white fleck

carrying resin scent
the wheelbarrow
with chopped wood

thick rime
just as warm the shabby
wool sweater

San Francisco cable car
Cinderella high heel shoe
came off downhill

garden Babel
the motley crowd of Zinnia
Thumbelina

soft breeze through acacia
the turtle got its house
full of flowers

fighting boredom my metrical foot

succulents—
propagating joy
my art

peacock train rattling—
in the wedding gift
a couple of feathers

cheese emporium
getting fond of
the stinky

learning joy from Vivaldi

herbarium
scents of many
summers

smiling Buddha
fitting in my palm—
I smile back

inner journey
wild longing
not found

picnic with friends
climbing a grass blade
a ladybug

Mother's Day
baby's breath bouquet
from the first born

first pregnancy
time for her
to blossom

between late frosts
cherry blossom
truce

old garden charm–
on her hands
new brown spots

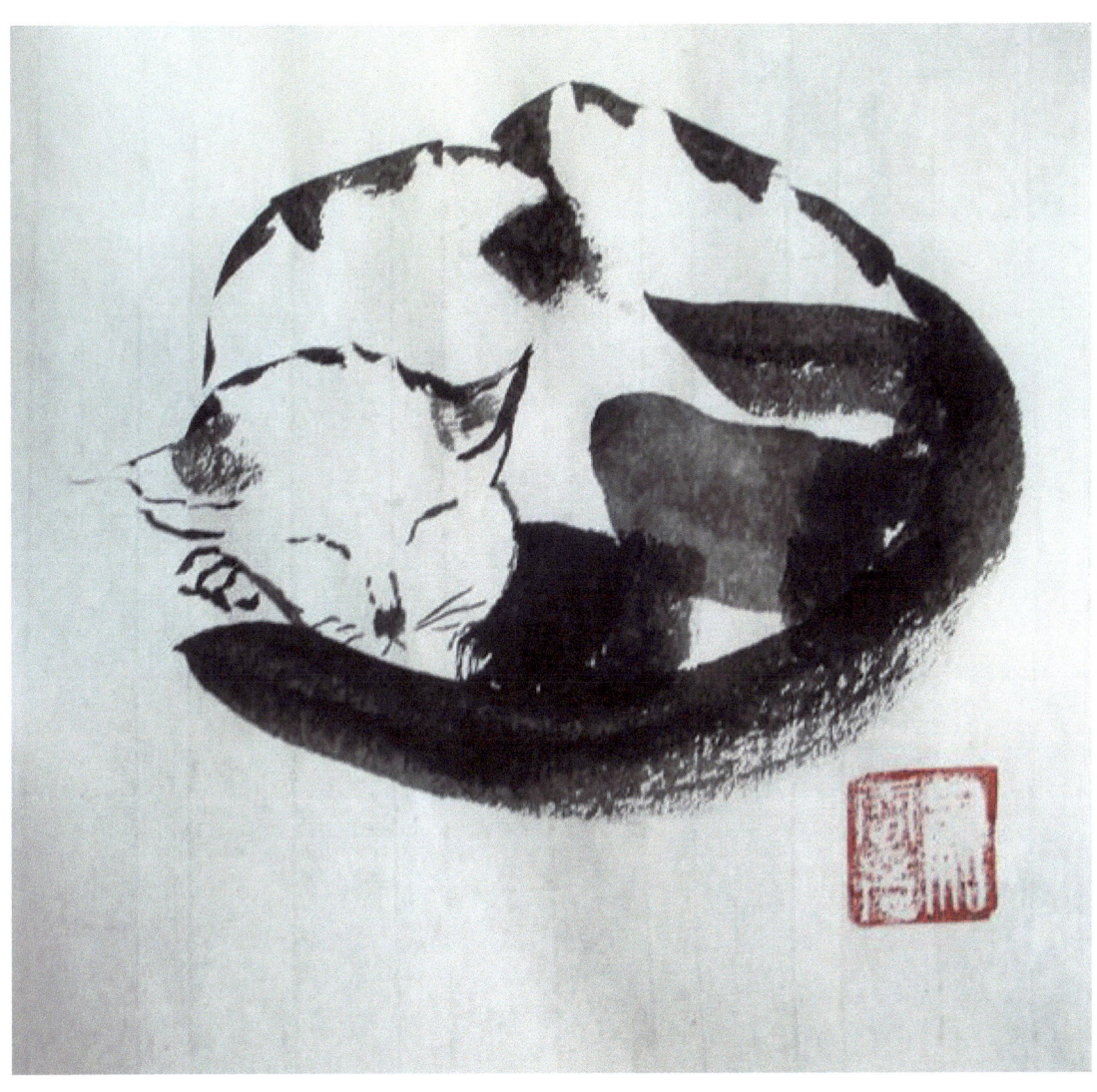